THE HOW AND WHY WONDER BOOK OF
ECOLOGY

Written by Shelly and Mary Louise Grossman
Photographs by Shelly Grossman

GROSSET & DUNLAP • Publishers • NEW YORK
A NATIONAL GENERAL COMPANY

Contents

	Page
THE CHAIN OF LIFE	3
How do plants eat?	4
What is a food chain?	4
Why must hawks eat more than butterflies do?	5
THE HABITATS	6
How are habitats connected?	10
What are the requirements of territories?	11
What is competition?	12
How did the ice ages affect life on earth?	12
What causes migration?	14
Why is hibernation necessary?	14
What do biological clocks tell animals?	14
THE SEASONS	16
When does spring begin?	16
THE BIOMES	17
What is a biome?	17
THE EASTERN FORESTS	18
Why did the passenger pigeon become extinct?	18
What is a niche?	19
Why is the decay of a tree important to a forest?	19
Why can different birds co-exist in a forest?	19
How do owls catch their prey?	20
THE GRASSLANDS	21
Why are plains treeless?	22
How have the grasslands changed?	22
What happened to the ducks?	23
How are coyotes killed?	24
How do prairie dogs protect themselves from enemies?	24
What is "the balance of nature"?	25
How is the balance destroyed?	25
Why is the black-footed ferret becoming extinct?	26
THE HOT DESERTS	27
How many deserts are in the Southwest?	27
How hot can a desert get?	27
How much rain does a desert get in a year?	28
What kind of plants grow in deserts?	28
Where do the birds of the desert nest?	29
How do birds get water?	30
How is the saguaro cactus able to store water?	30
Why does the sidewinder move the way it does?	31
What is the sidewinder's most deadly enemy?	31
How often must bighorn sheep drink in summer?	32

	Page
How are desert rodents able to live without drinking water?	32
How has the desert changed since the late 1800's?	33
THE COLD DESERT	34
What plant dominates the cold desert?	34
What happens to desert lakes when they dry up?	34
What was Pyramid Lake named for?	34
What has happened to Pyramid Lake?	35
Where do the pelicans have to feed in summer?	36
What does sonic boom do to the pelican eggs and babies?	36
THE MOUNTAINS	37
What does man take out of the mountains?	37
When did the Western mountains start to rise?	38
When were the last volcanic eruptions in the West?	38
What is the tundra?	39
Why are ptarmigan able to live here all year?	39
What else do eagles hunt on the tundra?	40
How does the pika prepare for winter?	40
How does the marmot spend the winter?	40
What is treeline?	40
Why are the evergreens at treeline small?	41
How do aspen trees grow?	41
What happens to a forest when it is lumbered?	41
What happens to a forest when trees fall naturally?	42
THE COASTLINES	42
How do coastlines vary?	42
How many tidal life zones are there?	42
What is a lichen?	43
How do acorn barnacles feed?	43
What is symbiosis?	44
Why are coastlines rich in life?	44
Why are we losing our fish supply?	44
Why are pesticides not working?	45
PROBLEMS AND ALTERNATIVES	45
How does DDT spread through food chains?	45
What is happening to birds' eggshells?	46
What is happening to pelicans in the U.S.?	46
What effect is DDT having on seals?	46
What is biological control?	47
What does a parasite do?	47
Does biological control work?	47
What can we do to stop pollution?	48

Library of Congress Catalog Card Number: 70-158768

ISBN: 0-448-04070-0 (Trade Edition)
ISBN: 0-448-03863-3 (Library Edition)

Copyright © 1971 by Shelly Grossman.
All rights reserved under International and Pan-American Copyright Conventions.
Published simultaneously in Canada.   Printed in the United States of America.

The Chain of Life

June in Florida. The low, slanting rays of the early morning sun force their way through the Spanish moss, draped over a thick branch of a live oak tree. Suddenly the stillness is interrupted by the incessant, high-pitched calling of three downy young red-tailed hawks, barely able to stand up in the nest. The young are calling for their breakfast. The parents, perched on a branch above the nest, were up before the sun, searching the ground for anything that moves. During this season of new birth, the adults must feed themselves and their young very often.

Red-tailed hawks eat mostly mice and rats, but they will try for almost anything that is easy to catch. Their nest is on a farm that belongs to a rancher who keeps pheasants, and like most men, he feels that everything on his ranch belongs to him. Even the hawks. So when the hawks kill some of his pheasants, he becomes angry. If he can find the nest, he will kill them. But this doesn't solve his problem. He will continue to lose pheasants, and not know why.

All things in nature are tied together, linked in an invisible chain of life. The rancher cannot break one of these links without affecting another. When a hawk — one of the links — is removed, its absence has an effect on all the other links. Mice, another link, are the natural food of the hawks. Killing the predatory hawk only makes it possible for more mice to survive. Greater numbers of these rodents eat more food, and when the grass and seed are all eaten up, they start in on other plants and the

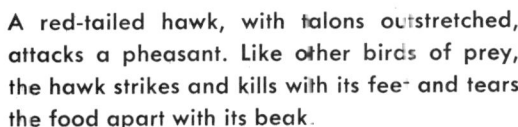

A red-tailed hawk, with talons outstretched, attacks a pheasant. Like other birds of prey, the hawk strikes and kills with its feet and tears the food apart with its beak.

bark of trees. So, unchecked by predators, the rodent population may leave the area barren. This affects the pheasants. First they lose their food supply, which is seed. Then they lose their protective cover. They have no place to hide from the other predators — the raccoons, the foxes, the bobcats and the weasels that now come in for a pheasant dinner. The rancher can now lose his entire flock. All of the links in this chain of life are necessary for survival in the environment.

How do plants eat? Life on earth starts with the sun, whose energy powers our planet. Traveling some 93,000,000 miles through space, some of the sun's rays are trapped in the earth's atmosphere. These rays are, in a way, food for plant life and for everything that eats plants. Aided by chlorophyll, the green pigment in the leaves, a plant combines solar energy with carbon dioxide taken from the air and water brought up by the roots, to manufacture sugars, starches, and possibly proteins and other materials vital to its life and growth. The whole process is called photosynthesis. The by-product, oxygen, then becomes available for animals to breathe. (And when they breathe, oxidation of food — the reverse of photosynthesis — takes place, releasing energy and making possible all of their life functions such as heat production, movement and growth.) Food energy produced by the plants passes to an animal when the vegetation is eaten, and passes again when the animal is killed and eaten by another. The energy flow

A zebra swallowtail butterfly sips nectar . . .

through this *food chain* can even be traced, by marking organisms with radioactive materials, and measured, by calculating the known rates at which oxygen is given off by plants and used up by animals.

What is a food chain? A food chain can be as simple as a plant being eaten by a cow, or as complicated as the one shown here. *Link number one:* A zebra swallowtail butterfly takes nectar from a flower in order to live. Some of the sun's energy has been transferred from the plant to the butterfly. *Link number two:* A predatory insect, the dragonfly, captures the butterfly, thereby getting some of the original energy which the butterfly received from the plant. *Link number three:* While at rest on a pickerel weed, digesting its food, the dragonfly is caught by a bullfrog. Some of the energy passed to the butterfly, to the dragonfly, now goes to the frog. *Link number four:* A snake captures the frog. *Link number five:* In the final act of our energy play, a red-shouldered hawk attacks and carries off the snake, and with it, a small part of the original energy of the sun, which has traveled 93,000,000 miles to get to the earth.

A dragonfly catches the butterfly...

A bullfrog eats the dragonfly...

A snake captures the bullfrog...

A FOOD CHAIN

On a Florida river, the lives of all these animals are linked by the chain of events in which one is eaten by another. It is in this way that energy passes through the community.

A red-shouldered hawk flies off with the snake in its talons.

While the butterfly may only have to sip nectar from a few flowers to sustain its life, the dragonfly may have to eat ten or more butterflies or other insects during the day to keep itself alive. The frog may have to catch dozens of insects and even smaller frogs during the evening and nighttime hours in order to live. The snake will devour many small animals, day and night, to sustain its life. The hawk, being the top predator in this food chain, must eat the most to stay alive — not just because the hawk is bigger than the butterfly, or any of the other links in the food chain, but because the original energy that was in the flower has been mostly used up, in the transference from animal to animal, as it has passed along the food chain.

Why must hawks eat more than butterflies do?

The Habitats

Cypress trees rooted in water are draped with Spanish moss, an air plant. These streamers absorb surface water and minerals from the bark after a downpour without harming the trees.

The red-shouldered hawk and all the other animals in this food chain live along the Weeki Wachee River, fed by a great underground spring in west-central Florida. It is not a very big river, winding only twelve miles from its source to the Gulf of Mexico. In this short distance its crystal-clear waters flow through many different kinds of *habitats*.

Around the spring itself grow tall cypress and smaller bay trees which are rooted in the water. (The bay leaf is the same one used as a seasoning in cooking.) Because of the overhanging branches, braided with lliana vines, and thick sheets of Spanish moss, the appearance of this part of the river is eerie and junglelike. There are many sounds, but it's hard to see where they come from. Certainly not from the egrets standing tall and silent along the river's edge. They are stalking, necks outstretched and long sharp beaks poised to snap up some unwary bream that happens to swim by. Alligators, sunning themselves on the bank, resemble logs until something causes them to slip off with scarcely an audible splash. Where the trees open and the water is shallow, a raccoon might venture out of cover long enough to try its luck with a school of passing minnows.

Like a submarine, the anhinga or snakebird, rises right up out of the clear water — periscopic neck first. If you keep watching, you'll see this bird dive again and again, finally coming up with a fish. The anhinga spears its prey with a sharp beak, barbed on the end for extra holding power. The fish is flipped and swallowed headfirst so that its spines lie flat and do not rip the bird's throat.

Along the sandy bank of the river, mud dauber wasps are collecting material to build their egg cells. The balls of mud are heavier than the wasps. But once the insects are airborne — launched from the top of the embankment — they can carry their burdens for at least a quarter of a mile to the place where the cells are being constructed. Once the cell has been nearly completed, the wasp has to catch and immobilize a spider with its poisonous sting. After being carried back to the cell, the stunned spider is incarcerated with a wasp egg that will later hatch, and the larva will have a live spider to eat.

Downstream, the jungle fades away and the river widens into fields of freshwater sawgrass. On the stalks of this grass, the nymphs of dragonflies climb up during the spring and transform into adults. They generally do this at night, when the sharp-eyed blackbirds and grackles won't see them. By dawn, the soft bodies of the newborn insects have hardened, and they fly away on strong wings, leaving only shells behind. As for the birds, their protection is the sea of grass itself. Their nests are hidden from coons and other predators, who must search the vastness with great care to find the eggs and young.

The anhinga, a diving bird, comes up with a fish.

Approaching the Gulf, salt and fresh water mix and wiregrass grows in the brackish water. Now the noises and calls of the birds are easier to identify. Instead of one or two egrets, dozens of wading birds gather in the shallow inlets where the current slackens and the pools are full of minnows. Among those hunting for their dinners are Louisiana herons, little blue herons, black-crowned night herons, snowy egrets, green herons, common herons — all stabbing into the water with their long, pointed beaks. All seeking the same kinds of fish, but in different ways. Consequently there is a minimum of squabbling and competition amongst the different species.

The little green heron with its short legs must station itself along the bank and grab. Its long neck and bill shoot out at passing prey with deadly precision. The snowy egret stays close to shore, while the taller, longer-legged Louisiana heron and common egret can venture out in the deeper water to fish. Another fish-eater, the black-crowned night heron, varies its diet by visiting the intertidal zone of the mud flats or sand beaches, waiting quietly to snatch up tiny fiddler crabs as they come out of their holes.

Entrenched in their Gulf-front homes, the fiddler crabs are so-called because the males habitually clean and polish one large claw with a small one, the "fiddle" played by the "bow." Or so someone thought who sat and watched, like hundreds of people afterwards — fascinated by this Lilliputian society. (A large fiddler crab might be an inch across.)

Since there are no plant-eaters to harvest the grasses of the marsh as a cow grazes in a pasture, most of the nutrients come from decayed grass and the principal scavengers happen to be these inconspicuous little fiddlers. They

Two male fiddler crabs lock claws in a fight over the occupancy of a burrow. In a situation like this, the owner of the burrow usually drives the challenger away.

In the shallow, brackish water of the coastal salt marsh, greater flocks of American egrets, herons, and other wading birds feed on minnows, shrimps, and crabs.

Male fiddler crab, life-size. His big claw is on the left side, but many are "right-handed" also.

turn the dead matter into a form that herons and many other predators can use.

They also eat dead fish and anything else they can find. At low tide these beautiful multicolored crabs gather in hordes along the receding waterline. A strange crackling noise fills the air as they sift the sand for particles of food. Around a dead fish, the males will use their big claw to defend their feeding station from others. There is much pushing and jousting, with each one trying to dislodge a neighbor from its chosen spot. The large claws lock and twist and turn, till one crab falls off. The winner continues to eat, only to be interrupted by another challenger. This kind of competition also goes on between the crabs in defense of their burrows. If for any reason a crab loses its hole, this homeless individual will try to capture the burrow of another crab. The fiddle claw is again used as a weapon. The invader wields it like a club, and the defender in the burrow uses it to block its entrance.

But the most important use of the fiddle claw is sexual. (Females have no fiddles — just two small feeding claws.) During the breeding season, the males attract females by signaling. At the appearance of a female, every male in sight will stand up high on its legs and wave the big claw. The closer the female comes to any of these individuals, the more agitated the claw-waving becomes, until the female finally follows one of the males down into his burrow, where they will mate.

When the tides come in, every six hours more or less, all the crabs take to their burrows and plug up the entrances with sand balls. Under the shallow sheet of salt water, not a ripple betrays the presence of the colony, which will only come alive on the ebb of the flow. Then, there will be a new deposit of edible things from the river and the Gulf.

How are habitats connected?

Every habitat through which the Weeki Wachee River flows is in some way connected by this thread of water. If for some reason the fresh water is polluted or the flow stopped, the brackish water in the marshes becomes too salty. The young of fishes and ocean shrimps may die. Fewer fishes would mean less food for fish-eating birds, and they would have trouble feeding and raising their young. The heronries in the trees upriver would be deserted. Eventually the whole river would be lifeless.

And because the tides are part of the life of the river, the dikes built by the housing developers on the Gulf pose another, imminent threat. The grass is destroyed by the dredging machines and replaced with a desert of limestone rock, and the sea walls block the ebb and flow of the salt water. Over acres and acres, there is nothing left — no place for the crabs to live, or the birds to come and feed.

Protected in the tangle of shrubbery surrounding their nest, young blue herons wait for their parents to return with fish. If the marsh is destroyed by man, the birds will lose both their living place and food supply.

What are the requirements of territories?

The most basic requirement of an animal is a place to live and an ample supply of food. This living space is called a *territory*. The red-shouldered hawk and the barred owl need trees of a certain size to nest, so you will only find them living in that part of the river forest which has the biggest cypress and bay. This woodland is extensive enough to house only one pair of red-shoulders and one pair of barred owls. These two predators do not compete with each other, even though they eat much the same food, because they hunt at different times — the hawk during the day, the owl at night.

From the river, they take fish, crayfish and frogs; from the land, they take rodents, snakes, shrews and small birds of many kinds. In fact, the list of prey is just about unlimited. The barred owls sometimes eat screech owls, which are about one-fourth their size.

The little screech owls also nest in the same woods, but they hunt mostly insects and some mice. Because they don't compete with the larger owls and occupy smaller trees, the same woodland space may accommodate several pairs.

The red-shouldered hawk, a daytime predator.

The barred owl, a nighttime predator.

A few hundred feet from the moist river bank, pines grow on the higher and drier sand ridges. Although there are no hollows in the evergreens for the owls, the red-shouldered hawks may build another nest in one of the tall spires next year. They move around the territory from season to season. And the barred owls, which do not build a nest, often prefer to move into the hawks' deserted quarters.

Other neighbors in the pines might be one or two pairs of sharp-shinned hawks. They're smaller and more secretive than the red-shoulders, and spend most of their time pursuing birds. Their especially long tails seem perfectly designed for fast turns in flight through tree trunks and branches.

In the surrounding woods outside the territory of these resident predators, there are other juvenile or single adult hawks and owls. They're sitting on the sidelines, in a manner of speaking. In some instances, the predatory birds need two or three years to mature and seek out their mates. If one of a pair of hawks or owls is killed, one of the bench-sitters of the appropriate sex will be accepted into the territory to fulfill the dead bird's duties.

What is competition? Although the woods may be both a hunting and nesting territory for these hawks and owls, some maintain nests far from the places they hunt. It depends on the circumstances. But the hunting grounds are shared with other, non-competitive species. Wherever animals *do* compete with each other for either food or living places, someone must be driven out; there is just not enough for two families of the same species.

How did the ice ages affect life on earth? Millions of years ago, much of the land mass that was North America resembled the area around the Weeki Wachee River in Florida. There were great marshy tracts. The climate was mild. There was an abundance of tropical and sub-tropical life. (Palms and alligators as far North as the Dakotas; magnolias and figs in Alaska.) Then something hap-

Sperry Glacier, a remnant of the ice ages in northern Montana. Peaks of the Continental Divide in the background were sculptured thousands of years ago by ice that once filled the valley.

pened about 135 million years ago. Gradually, the climate cooled and the land began to change. Mountain chains emerged in the West. Their seaward slopes caught the coastal wind and rain, creating arid regions inland. Deserts in the Southwest and Great Plains in the center of the continent, instead of swamps. Gradually the polar ice caps formed, and during four great glacial periods nearly a third of the land was scoured by ice sheets thousands of feet thick. During the advances and retreats of the ice, untold numbers of plants and animals became extinct — unable to adapt to the changes. Only 12,000 years ago, the last ice sheet began to melt. From their southern survival centers, trees and other plants returned to the barren northern landscape — their seeds carried on the winds and river currents. First the hardy evergreens with leaves rolled into needles, which effectively protected their surfaces against drought or freezing. Then, as the soil improved, the deciduous trees that lose their leaves in preparation for a season of rest, or cold weather. The animals moved as far North as they could, and still withstand the winters. For the most part, they hibernated or had to dig their food out from under the snow. Birds migrated South, and so did some species of insects, to avoid the cold. Many insects lived only one season anyway, but laid eggs that could winter over and hatch the next spring. Others sought protection under the bark of trees or underground — whichever the varied forms of their entire life cycles would allow — as egg, pupa, larva, or adult.

What causes migration? The triggering mechanisms for migration and hibernation have just recently been discovered. Many animals (and plants, too) have a way of measuring and comparing the daylight hours or photoperiod; they do not respond to the short days of the fall, but as the days lengthen in late winter and spring, certain physiological changes take place. Not all of the details of this "biological clock" have been worked out, but a bird knows it is time to migrate back to its Northern nesting grounds when the days become longer. Scientists believe that this information is received through the eyes and triggers the manufacture of hormones that activate the reproductive organs, fat deposition necessary for the trip, and migratory restlessness. The whole cycle is likened to a clock constantly rewound by the recurrence of short days. Because temperature and weather vary considerably from year to year, day length is the most reliable guide to the season of the year. In plants, growth and flowering may be controlled by photoperiod, acting through a pigment called phytochrome.

Why is hibernation necessary? Among the living organisms least affected by daylight in this way are reptiles, amphibians and insects that sleep through the winter. They are cold-blooded — that is, their bodies are generally about the same temperature as the air because of inability to generate or regulate body heat as a bird or mammal does. If a snake is too cold, for example, it won't move or feed. It will only wake up and come out of its winter den when the outside air temperature reaches 50 degrees F.

But the woodchuck has a biological clock, set for the spring season. From a state of hibernation during which this animal has a heart rate of four beats a minute and a body temperature of 38 degrees F., he can in four hours involuntarily raise his heart rate up to 75 beats a minute and his temperature up to 98 degrees F. So if the woodchuck ventures out on Ground Hog Day, February 2, and sees that it's still winter, he will go back to sleep for a few more days or weeks. If, however, he happens to wake during a thaw and can find something to eat, he may just stay up to look for a mate. He's primarily programmed to wake up at a certain time of year (though not necessarily February 2), and secondarily influenced by temperature and food supply.

What do biological clocks tell animals? No one knows how far back in geological time these biological clocks go, but they probably evolved in response to drastic ice age climate changes, when

A white-crowned sparrow in the willows of the Alaskan tundra. Here this bird has an unusual cycle of activity. Because there is daylight almost twenty-four hours a day during the nesting season, there seems to be no particular time for sleeping or feeding. Thus it is done sporadically, throughout the day.

conditions became unfavorable for many plants and animals in the North, and some way of telling the time of year — some way of knowing when to migrate or hibernate — was absolutely essential for survival.

Over the millennia, the system has worked. Regardless of the weather, December 21 is invariably a shorter day than June 21 — of any year, in the Northern Hemisphere.

On its wintering grounds in Southern California, the white-crowned sparrow is prepared for migration to Alaska by the increasing hours of daylight during April. The biological clock tells the bird that it's time to molt into breeding plumage. It releases hormones into the bloodstream that increase the size of the gonads and start the breeding cycle. And when conditions are right, the sparrow will start north. All this is designed to get the bird back to its nesting area when the snow has melted and food is available for a nesting pair and their babies.

After the 21st of June, as the days begin to get shorter, and the young are out of the nest, something happens to them internally. Families fly around in groups, developing their wing muscles, and as the daylight continues to diminish, the groups become larger. Great flocks of sparrows start their migration south, long before their food supply is gone, and long before the snows fall.

In the long view of nature, plants and animals have attempted to colonize every possible place on earth. Some fail, some succeed. But all are governed by the seasons, which are most rigorous in the temperate zones.

The Seasons

At six thousand feet in the Montana Rockies, fireweed is a late spring or early summer flower. At this elevation, the blazing pink fields signal the start of about eight weeks of summer.

When does spring begin?

In North America, spring — the season of rebirth — has many faces and does not necessarily appear on schedule, as marked on the calendar. In the southern part of Florida around the Everglades, spring flowers bloom in January. The many water birds, egrets and herons, bald eagles and ospreys, begin their courtships then, and fight their neighbors for nesting sites in the mangroves. By February there will be eggs and babies in the nests, even though the rest of the country is still locked in freezing cold and anticipating more months of winter. Spring in the deserts of the

Southwest (Arizona and New Mexico) is just a few weeks behind Florida's. By mid-February and March, the land is a riot of color. Brittlebush, poppy, lupine and other desert plants create a psychedelic carpet unsurpassed anywhere — if there have been winter rains. The dozens of species of cacti bloom later, in April and May.

Spring, however, does begin in mid-March in the Northeast while there is still snow on the ground in the Eastern forests. The first flowers to poke their heads through the melting snow are the reddish-purple cowls of the skunk cabbage. The red color of the plant absorbs the rays of the sun and the heat actually melts the surrounding snow. Meanwhile, the buds of bloodroot, wood anemone and hepaticas are protected under leaf litter that is ten degrees warmer than the outside world.

In the Western mountains, spring must wait until the sun is high enough above the peaks so that the rays reach the valley floors and the snows begin to melt. Here, too, early spring flowers like the pasque flower are red or purple-colored, and this one is also furry—another device to keep warm. It has been said that spring advances up the side of a mountain at the rate of about a hundred feet a day. You can select any flower and check out the theory. For example, the pasque flowers that bloom in April at 6,000 feet in the Colorado Rockies will have died and gone to seed by the time the same kind of flower begins to bloom in May at 9,000 to 10,000 feet in the same mountains. At 12,000 feet and higher in the Rockies, spring practically merges with summer because the blooming season starts at the end of June or early in July. Above treeline, the tundra growing season is extremely short. In some places, this period may last only twenty-eight days.

So spring does not occur on the 21st of March across the continent, even though the calendar says it does.

The Biomes

What is a biome?

As spring varies across this vast land, so does the land itself. There are coastlines and forests, grasslands and deserts, and mountains. These areas have evolved different flora and fauna, depending on the climate, rainfall and type of soils, and are called *biomes*.

The science of ecology attempts to show us how all the *habitats* of every *biome* fit together, each one with a unique combination of living organisms, in a kind of natural history jigsaw puzzle. If we lose some of the pieces of our jigsaw puzzle, we can never hope to see the whole picture . . . and ecology *is* the whole picture. We can start to put our puzzle together in the year 1500, before European man set foot on the North American continent.

A white-tailed buck with antlers in velvet. Since colonial days, many parts of the Eastern forest have become overpopulated with deer, which eat up the shrubbery and damage the trees. Finally, the deer starve to death, especially in winter. This happens because no wolves, mountain lions, or other large predators are left to help control their numbers.

Mixed Coniferous and Deciduous Forest

The Eastern Forests

In 1500, the eastern part of North America was covered with a great forest. Indians were hunting wild turkey, deer, many species of birds, wolves and mountain lions at the time that Verrazano, Champlain, Cartier and other explorers reached these shores. They literally came from another world — Europe, which had been lumbered over by the end of the 11th century. So they believed that they had found Eden, a "virgin" place. They saw almost four times as many different species of trees as could be found in their homelands. That was the way the New World was in the 1500's. By 1830, about 80 to 90 per cent of these forests were gone from New England — lumbered for homes and ship masts, cleared for farms.

Why did the passenger pigeon become extinct?

In 1870, hundreds of square miles of beech forest in Wisconsin — some of the last of these mid-Western tracts — housed the nests of thousands of passenger pigeons, some of the last of this species. Thirty years later when the beech forests fell to the woodsman's ax, the pigeons became extinct. Most incredible was the fact that these birds had numbered in the billions throughout the East. Just a few years before the crash, the supply seemed limitless. But a species cannot exist if its requirements for life are removed. Passenger pigeons needed the forests for shelter and food, and both these elements were taken from them. The other irony was that the Carolina parakeet—almost as plentiful in the coastal forests in former years — became extinct in the very same year, 1914.

Though the animal life has changed, some remnants of the "virgin" forest can be seen today, mostly in the Great Smoky Mountains of North Carolina and Tennessee. In the valleys or "coves" of the Smokies stand giant oaks, hickories, tulips, bass, walnuts and other deciduous trees. Cathedral-like, their trunks reach more than a hundred feet high and are covered by lacy canopies. This deciduous woodland, mixed with evergreens, once spread from Maine to the northern part of Georgia; from the Atlantic Coast to mid-continent. There were always more kinds of trees — and bigger ones—here because of the heavy rainfall, up to 100 inches compared to a minimum of 28 inches and a maximum of 60 inches in other places.

Certain combinations of trees and other plants attract particular animals. Gray squirrels have a preference for the oak-hickory forest because they feed on acorns and hickory nuts. Red squirrels inhabit forests where pines are numerous because of their preference for pine cone seeds. Each has its *niche,* its occupation in the habitat.

What is a niche?

The forest habitat is a multi-layered world in which flowers and shrubs are dominated, literally overshadowed, by trees. Even the trees compete with each other. In an oak-beech forest, where almost 90 per cent of the sunlight is screened out by the foliage of these predominant trees, only red maple, hickory and other shade-loving plants can exist in the understory. The competition continues underground as the root systems vie for water and nutrients and ground space.

When an old tree falls, new spaces are created and new niches for all kinds of life. Like the fallen leaves, which form a thick mulch on the ground, the wood returns to the soil and recycles minerals. It does this, not all at once, but in a series of steps that differ according to the conditions. Many kinds of fungi and lichens penetrate and soften the surface of the dead tree. Beetles, termites and carpenter ants can then move in and attack the heartwood, and these insects provide food for a tiny shrew in the ground litter. One of the smallest living animals, the short-tailed shrew weighs less than an ounce, and eats three times its weight in insects each day.

Why is the decay of a tree important to a forest?

The opening in the forest canopy allows sunlight to penetrate and shrubs start to grow in greater profusion on the forest floor. This new growth allows deer, which are browsers (eaters of shrubs), to come into the habitat in greater numbers. Deer generally feed at the forest's edge.

With the increase in brush come the insects that feed on this type of foliage, and birds that hunt the insects, or gather the seeds and berries. A number of warblers can live in the same woods and not compete with each other

Why can different birds co-exist in a forest?

19

because they all have different niches, which keep them at different levels of the bushes and trees.

Chestnut-sided warblers hunt the insects of the shrubbery, while higher up, the redstarts pick off the caterpillars hanging from the branches of the trees. Still higher, in the treetops, Blackburnian warblers catch insects on the wing. All three species nest on the same levels where they hunt their prey. Consequently, their occupations are limited to the levels on which they live. They have relatively narrow niches in the entire forest complex.

Not so the great horned owl and other large predatory birds. The owl nests up high, either in the hollow of a dead tree or the unoccupied nest of a hawk. Its hunting expeditions are not restricted to any particular level. It has a broad niche in the habitat, affecting the lives of snake, bird and mammal — nearly anything that moves.

How do owls catch their prey? Although the great horned owl may be out during the daytime, this bird shares with other owls the ability to hunt by sound rather than sight. It can catch prey in total darkness. So, while the shrew is out at night looking for insects in the forest floor, the owl above may hear the rustling of leaves. Having determined the location of the prey by sound alone, the owl descends on soft, fluffy wing feathers — as though parachuted down — and strikes with deadly accuracy.

When the rich prairie lands to the West were opened to the homesteaders in the late 1800's, the hilly New England farms were abandoned. Today, more than 60 per cent of these farms have become woods again. The sounds of warblers and pileated woodpeckers can be heard again. But this second-growth forest is not the same forest of 1500.

Death comes to a bull snake. The great horned owl's talons grasp its coils and thoroughly puncture the reptile while its head is torn by the bird's sharp beak.

You can discern which owls are mostly out at night by the extent of the heart-shaped facial disc. The barn owl (left) is heard more often than seen because of its completely nocturnal habits. The barred owl (center) could be seen hunting on cloudy days. The screech owl (right) may be abroad day or night. The most nocturnal hunter needs the biggest facial disc of special "filo" feathers, which are sound receptors and help the bird locate its prey in darkness.

The Grasslands

Nor is the treeless grassland, or prairie, the biome on the western edge of the forest, the same today as the scene described by Spanish explorers who visited Kansas in the 1540's. At that time, some 60,000,000 bison or buffalo roamed this land, from Montana down along the Rockies and south to Texas, and across the entire mid-continent to the forests of Pennsylvania and Kentucky.

Ecologically, the bison were necessary for the survival of the many grasses that once grew on the plains. These plants could only renew themselves because their seeds were crushed open by

Bull buffalo, or bison, weigh up to two thousand pounds. They roam today only in a few parks and refuges, or on private ranches. The combined herds of Wind Cave National Park and Custer State Park, in the Black Hills of South Dakota, number about 1,500, the largest in the country.

the hoofs of the bison on their annual migrations. These herds traveled across the country at a leisurely pace of about four to five miles an hour, moving north in the summer and south in the winter. The great numbers of bison, grazing on all the varied grasses, apparently did little damage to the land because of these yearly movements. By not staying in one place for any long periods of time, the herds allowed the grasses to grow back.

Why are plains treeless?

The Great Plains are deceptively flat-looking. Actually, from where they start on the eastern edge of Kansas, at an elevation of less than a thousand feet above sea level, to the Front Range of the Rockies, about 550 miles away, the land slopes upward gently to mile-high Denver. The average yearly rainfall across this expanse is about 20 inches. The eastern edge in Kansas garners more rain than the Rocky Mountain side. The mountains act as a barrier, stopping the moist Pacific air from ever reaching the prairies. Without sufficient rainfall, trees cannot grow on the plains. But that's just one reason why the plains are treeless.

The grass mat that covered the plains at one time was so thick that few seedling trees could grow there, and hard pan clay underneath also made life for trees with deep taproots impossible. There are some, mostly cottonwoods, on the flood plains of the many rivers that dissect this grassy world, and along the creeks.

Grasses adapt very nicely to a meager supply of rainfall. The roots braid themselves together very thickly and burrow down more than eight feet to reach ground water. They often travel by runners — endless miles of roots that capture any available moisture. In an experiment, one rye grass plant grew 378 miles of roots in just four months. The deep or extensive root systems of prairie grasses can survive the numerous lightning fires that occur during the late spring and summer months — fires that easily destroy any "pioneer" trees.

How have the grasslands changed?

Many things have happened in the past hundred years to change the grasslands forever. Buffalo hunters and the U.S. Army slaughtered the bison herds, the main food supply of the Plains Indians. By 1900, the 60,000,000 bison that once roamed the continent were almost wiped out. Finally, only 21 wild bison were left in the entire United States. And the

The delicate, graceful pronghorn antelope is not restricted to refuges. It can be seen throughout the ranch country of the West.

Plains Indians were subdued along with their buffalo brothers. Cattle and sheep invaded the land by the thousands, sent to replace the bison for commercial reasons. But the ecology differed — although the buffalo roamed freely across half a continent, allowing the varied grasses to renew themselves, the new owners of the land fenced the pastures. The domestic animals stayed in one place, eating the grasses and then the roots. The land was destroyed and the soil eroded.

Those areas of the plains that were plowed up by the homesteaders who deserted the rocky hillsides of the East for the rich "free" land of the West suffered another sickness. Hundreds of thousands of acres of crops were planted. As long as there was rain, the homesteaders thrived. The land was healthy. But then, in the 1930's, there was drought. Without the thick mat of grass, the topsoil blew away.

When the farmers ripped up the soil to replace the grasses with cultivated stands of wheat, rye, barley and oats (which are varieties of wild grasses), they created problems for themselves that have still not been solved. A single large crop of wheat attracts incredible numbers of insects that regard this bounty as a feast. To protect the wheat, the farmer must spray poison over the land and try to kill the insects. As if that is not enough, the plowing of the plains breaks up the thick mat of grasses, and the dust storms that result are testimony to the fact that the original plants held the land together — but the crops do not, and in the dry periods, much of the prairie is unusable by man or animal.

What happened to the ducks?

Myriad ponds or "potholes" from the last glacial melt-off dotted the northern prairies when the white man settled there. Uncounted flocks of ducks and other waterfowl reared their young in these prairie waters. Then farm machinery was invented that increased the amount of work a farmer could do, and the land he could till. So he drained the potholes to increase his acreage. Reclamation of potholes started in Iowa and Nebraska, and then spread to Minnesota, Nebraska, the Dakotas and Canada. Assisted by funds from the U.S. Government, the drainage that began in the 1930's, and accelerated during the Second World War, eliminated half of the farm ponds that once covered 115,000 square miles and supported at least 15,000,000 ducks.

When it was found that the duck population below the Canadian border had dropped to fewer than 5,000,000, in 1962, the Department of Agriculture decided to rectify the mistake. It now pays farmers up to 50 per cent of the cost of restoring wildlife habitats on farms, including the ponds.

Who cared about the ducks? The conservationists, of course; the hunters, particularly. It was largely through the efforts of Ducks Unlimited, an organization of hunters who feared the end of the duck-shooting in the great waterfowl wintering grounds of the Mississippi Delta, that funds have been made available and channeled to save wetlands. Thousands of acres now have been subsidized, or bought with Federal, state and private funds.

How are coyotes killed?

Though the land may be reclaimed successfully, and some wildlife restored by this kind of management, the total ecology of the grasslands can never be as it was before the farmer and rancher came. These new landlords have exterminated the wolves. They have hunted the coyotes down from airplanes or with poisoned baits or with a device called a coyote-getter that shoots a bullet of cyanide into the mouth when the animal pulls on the trigger — a scented tallow tip. One of the oldest methods, the steel trap, is also still in use. And as if all this killing isn't enough, the ranchers have conducted extermination campaigns against the rodents — the natural prey of the coyotes.

In the 1930's, the U.S. Government poisoned out many of the vast prairie dog towns in Kansas, Nebraska and the Dakotas. At that time, these sociable little rodents *did* occupy enormous areas. (One of the biggest prairie dog towns is said to have been a hundred miles long and twenty miles wide.) Whether they were eating up all the grass, as the ranchers believed, is open to question, however. During a drought, there was just not enough grass for the wildlife or the livestock, and it was easy to blame the prairie dogs.

How do prairie dogs protect themselves from enemies?

The prairie dogs feed together freely, and have an elaborate system of communicating with each other. They are named for one special territorial call—a distinct "Yip"

Only the fittest survive — the coyote is a prime example. In 1966 alone, 77,258 of these animals were killed by government trappers.

— given while standing up on their hind legs and raising their front legs straight overhead. It means, more or less, "This is my house." When a predator comes, they take an entirely different attitude — crouching over their burrows, wagging their tails, and letting out a high-pitched warning call. This warning is relayed from animal to animal, the length and breadth of the town, until all have ducked into their burrows. Not until the hawk has flown by, or the family of coyotes has wandered through, will they all come out again. Of course, some animals can pursue them down into their burrows. Rattlesnakes hide in the holes, and sometimes kill and eat the young prairie dogs. (The adults aren't prey, because they're too big for the snakes to swallow. In fact, they're even aggressive toward the snake and will try to suffocate it by blocking up the hole, if possible.) A slender-bodied weasel, the black-footed ferret, makes an almost exclusive profession of raiding prairie dogs' holes. And the badger is strong enough to dig them out, even though many of the burrows are 20 feet deep.

But the prairie dog could cope with its natural predators; the elaborate social system of the town made survival possible through the centuries. And the predators even had a beneficial influence: they culled out the weak, the slow and the sick animals, and a certain number of the surplus young, which would otherwise have had to move out and form new towns.

What is "the balance of nature"?

For the most part, the number of dogs was probably held down by their various predators. Hawk, owl, bobcat, wolf, coyote, snake, badger and ferret existed along with the prairie dogs on the land in a kind of elastic equilibrium. Ecologists once described these relationships as "the balance of nature." Actually, the situation here and in any habitat is much more fluid than originally supposed, continually going in and out of balance depending on the weather and other natural factors, and on how much tampering man does.

A victim of its sociable habits — the prairie dog has been poisoned by the hundreds of millions since the 1930's.

The prairie rattlesnake, coiled to strike. It is attracted to its prey by motion and body warmth, detected by a special heat-sensing organ.

How is the balance destroyed?

Now that we have killed off many of the predators, for example, one predator such as a coyote or hawk cannot by itself have much effect on the population of a dog town on a rancher's property. The town will go on growing to the limit of the food supply — the wild flowers and grasses on the cattle range.

Man must become the predator on the prairie dogs . . . or so he thinks. He shoots some, for sport, but mostly poisons them in their burrows. This is easily done by dropping in strychnine or 1080-treated grain, and all the prairie dogs are soon dead. Their customary habit of living in communities is no longer a protection, but has lead to their tragic downfall.

In South Dakota there are some ranchers who have given up killing. They like to see the coyotes and the hawks, and by letting these predators come back to the land, they are restoring a part of the natural equilibrium. Gradually the predators take over the dog towns, which are much smaller now than in the old days. And man, to his surprise, finds that there is very little need for rodent control.

Why is the black-footed ferret becoming extinct?

One of the tragedies of mass prairie dog poisoning on the Great Plains was the discovery that the black-footed ferret is nearly extinct. A few years ago biologists of the Federal Government and the state of South Dakota found that the ferret lives only in prairie dog towns, its main food being the dogs. And with the disappearance of many of the prairie dog towns (outside of wildlife preserves), these rare weasels have declined, too. Probably fewer than a hundred of them now inhabit the entire plains — the total world population, which is restricted to North America.

Mostly out at night, if he's out at all, the black-footed ferret is difficult to find. He has a habit of storing away a meat supply of several prairie dogs and staying underground for days at a time.

The Hot Deserts

A common cactus, the chain-fruit cholla replants itself by dropping its fruit and parts of its branches.

How many deserts are in the Southwest?

To the southwest of the plains lies another vast treeless area, the hot desert biome. It's actually three regions: the Sonoran Desert of California, Arizona and Mexico; the Mojave Desert, just northward in California, Nevada and Arizona; and the Chihuahuan Desert of New Mexico, West Texas and Mexico.

How hot can a desert get?

These desert areas *are* hot, the Mojave having the distinction of recording the hottest temperature ever in North America — 134 degrees F. (The world record, in the Libyan Desert of North Africa, is 136 degrees F.) Generally the temperature in the summer lingers around 110 degrees F. during midday, and drops

27

into the 50's at night. Under the clear desert skies, the heat of the day rapidly dissipates as soon as the sun goes down.

Much of the desert *is* dry; that is, receives very little rainfall. The dictionary will tell you that a true desert receives less than six inches of rainfall a year — and what it does get may come as a drenching downpour, all at once. Average precipitation figures are deceptive, for some parts of the Mojave get as little as 1/100 of an inch of rain some years while in Southern Arizona the Sonoran Desert gets as much as 19 inches of rain. Since more rain means more plants and more animal life, the Arizona hillsides don't conform to most people's idea of a desert as a sandy or rocky place, relatively devoid of life. The Chihuahuan Desert gets more rain than the Mojave, but less than the Sonoran. And these differences make the three American deserts among the most unusual and diverse on earth. Their plants and animals, however, have one common problem: adaptation to the heat and lack of a regular water supply.

How much rain does a desert get in a year?

Starting with the trees: if you think of a tree as having a great main trunk with branches and green leaves, these deserts have very few. There is the paloverde, or "green stick" tree, that grows in the normally dry river beds. Some of the older ones are 30 or 40 feet high. There are smoke trees and cottonwoods near water, but the land is mostly claimed by cacti and other kinds of succulent (water-storing) plants. Each of the three areas has a particular kind of large cactus or succulent plant which is unique to that desert, and which for that reason is called an "indicator" plant.

What kind of plants grow in deserts?

In the Sonoran Desert, this characteristic plant is the saguaro cactus, which grows 30 to 40 feet high with branching arms that turn up to the sky. Many kinds of birds nest in the giant cactus as they would in an ordinary tree. The gila woodpecker, for example, drills the same kind of hole in the fleshy trunk as the Eastern woodpeckers do in oaks or beech trees. The branching arms of the cactus may cradle the nest of a red-tailed hawk. An abandoned woodpecker hole might house pygmy or elf owls.

The silhouette of the Sonoran Desert — saguaro cactus columns.

28

The twisted shapes of the Mojave — Joshua trees.

The king of the yuccas in the Chihuahuan Desert — giant dagger.

In the Mojave Desert, the saguaro cactus is replaced by the Joshua tree. Its name was bestowed by the Mormons in honor of that Biblical prophet because its branches have such a prayerful attitude. The Joshua tree is not a cactus, but a member of the yucca family. Unlike the saguaro, which blooms and bears bright red fruit every year, even if there is no rain, the Joshua tree may not bloom for years if there is no rain. It is pollinated by a moth which only emerges from its pupal state in the ground if there is enough winter rain.

Where do the birds of the desert nest?

The yuccas serve the bird life of the Mojave in much the same way as the giant cacti of Arizona. Ladder-back woodpeckers drill holes in the trunks for their nest, and when these holes are abandoned by the woodpeckers, the screech owls use them.

One indicator plant of the Chihuahuan Desert, the giant dagger, is also a member of the yucca family. It grows eight to ten feet tall, and its crown of thick, stiletto-shaped leaves may house the nest of the white-tailed hawk.

Many smaller cacti, like the cholla (*choya*), appear throughout the deserts. In these, cactus wrens are the first to weave their football-shaped nests. After the young wrens leave, the oval nest may be broken down by mourning doves and used by these birds for their later nesting. Still later in the season, roadrunners carry sticks and twigs to the chollas, poking them in between the thorny branches to make a broad, loose platform. These usually scrappy, noisy birds sit quietly during incubation, as do most of the birds that nest in the spiny fortresses. Though protected, they're also open to the ears and eyes of predators. (Snakes, which are deaf, look for movement.) During March, April and

May, a quarter of the continent's 800 species of birds make their homes in the Sonoran Desert. They can live in this water-poor area only because there are so many different habitats for nesting. From the cholla gardens on the bajada or outwash plains of the mountains, the cacti and shrubs sweep upward to altitudes of 8,000 to 10,000 feet — high enough and moist enough for pine forests that house jays, martins, ravens and hawks.

Birds get their water in various ways. **How do birds get water?** Hawks and owls obtain all they need from the bodies of the animals they eat. Seed-eaters, such as quail and doves, fly daily to numerous springs in the mountains to drink. Sparrows dig into the moist, fleshy cactus plants that abound throughout the desert, getting their supply from plants that horde water. Other birds consume insects, a prime source of moisture. And during the flowering season of the cacti — April and May — the blossoms provide much nectar, not only for birds, but also for insects and bats.

By the end of June and early July, the rainy season starts. **How is the saguaro cactus able to store water?** The sky is filled with clouds. Each day one can scan the immense horizon and see more and more dark clouds gathering in scattered places across the seemingly endless desert. Then the downpour comes. Water holes fill, and rivers, which have been dry for months, flood in minutes. A sheet of water engulfs the bajada on its way down from the mountains, and the dry arroyos (ditches) overflow. The shallow, widespread roots of the cacti drink up the water quickly, storing the precious moisture in their spongy bodies. If you examine a saguaro cactus, you will find that it is composed of a bundle of elastic ribs covered with a thick, fluted skin. This cactus can expand as it absorbs the water from the summer floods, storing the reserve for months. During years of little rain, the cactus shrinks.

Without all of the cactus plants that store water, there would be few nesting places for birds in the hot lowlands; less water would be available to the wildlife, ranging from the birds, bats and bees that sip the nectar of the flowers to the small mammals that eat the flesh and fruits.

The Sonoran Desert gets winter rain as well as the summer rains, and it is the winter rain or lack of it in some years that determines the extent of the spring flowering — which in some years is unbelievable.

The extent of this bloom will determine how many insects will be able to survive the new season, as the flowers provide the major food supply for the insects. The number of insects that survive will determine the population of birds and other animals that depend on the insects for food. All things are tied to the rhythm and cycle of the rainfall.

In years of poor rainfall, some seeds may lie dormant and not germinate. These seeds have chemicals in them that must be washed away by at least an inch of rain before they will sprout and embark upon a season of growth. In some parts of the desert, the flowers equipped with these rain gauges haven't been seen in a decade.

Why does the sidewinder move the way it does?

As the plants and birds have adjusted to this rhythm of heat and rainfall, so have the many mammals and reptiles which reside in the desert. The sidewinder rattlesnake moves across the hot sands of the desert floor by pushing its body forward in a kind of S-motion, with only two parts of the snake's body touching the ground at any one time. One reason for this is traction — it's an easy way for a legless animal to cross the sand. More importantly, however, the temperature of that sand may get as high as 180 degrees F. By moving rapidly and keeping nearly all of the body elevated just a few millimeters off the surface, the snake can move around without being scorched to death.

Mostly, however, animal activity goes on in the early morning, late afternoon or evening hours. In fact, the desert may get too cold for the snake's comfort during the night, which explains why the roads in sidewinder country attract so many of the reptiles. The hard-packed soil or pavement retains heat longer than the sandy areas nearby.

What is the sidewinder's most deadly enemy?

Though most rattlesnakes won't attack unless provoked, the little sidewinder is bold and peppery. So it's a good idea to look around carefully before you walk in the desert. The snakes rest during the day in some of the multitudes of holes dug by kangaroo rats and other small rodents, or stay tightly coiled — almost invisible — under bushes. About five o'clock in the afternoon, they are most active, looking for these rodents. The snakes

One of the smallest of the desert snakes, the sidewinder may grow to be eighteen inches long. Because it literally moves sideways with a looping motion of its coils, its trail is a series of parallel lines.

A strange snake-killer — the roadrunner. Having subdued the poisonous reptile, the bird will gradually swallow and digest it all. The swallowing process alone may take at least an hour.

have very few enemies, but one is particularly in the habit of going after them: the clownish roadrunner. This crow-sized bird puts on a snake dance designed to tire its prey. It attacks and retreats, attacks and retreats, always avoiding the snake's strike, until the time comes to close in and make the kill.

During the dry season, all of the larger mammals — the peccaries, deer, pronghorn antelopes and bighorn sheep — are concentrated around a few mountain streams and waterholes. There, bobcats and other predators may be lying in wait for them. Consequently, some of the herd animals — the sheep in particular — are so shy of any noise that they may leave without even putting their heads down to drink. Game wardens in the Federal refuges, who have established blinds at the waterholes and count the animals each year, report that in the hottest and driest weeks (during June or July) the wild sheep come in to drink at least once in five days.

How often must bighorn sheep drink in summer?

By contrast, the little kangaroo rat doesn't drink at all. It can eat the dry seeds of the desert and turn them into water within its own body. (One gram of carbohydrates in the seeds produces .6 gram of water when oxidized; fats and proteins are similarly converted.) The kangaroo rat also recycles its urine, through a special kidney, in a way that

How are desert rodents able to live without drinking water?

allows very little loss of water. As long as the kangaroo rat comes out to feed only at night, it gets along very well.

Other rodents, including the pocket mouse and antelope ground squirrel, also have specially adapted kidneys that reabsorb two to three times as much water as those of mice and squirrels living elsewhere.

Unlike these animals, man has no special adaptations for living in the desert. He has no way to manufacture or recycle water internally. Unfortunately, when he does live in the desert, it is mostly at the expense of the other animal life.

How has the desert changed since the late 1800's?

According to the historical evidence, the Southwestern deserts were quite different in the years before 1870. The land was less brushy — more grassy and swampy. Rivers ran that are now lost in the sands, except during the brief rains. In the streams of southern Arizona, salmon trout and beaver were abundant, and turkeys hatched out in waist-high grass. Today this kind of environment can be seen only around an oasis such as Quitobaquito, a one-and-a-half-acre pond in Organ Pipe National Monument.

For centuries, small tribes of Papagos, Yumas, and other desert Indians had lived in harmony with the land. They gathered the fruits of the cactus plants in the lowlands and hunted the game in the mountains.

Then, around 1700, the Spanish brought their herds of cattle and sheep over the Mexican border. They were followed by Mexican and Anglo cattlemen and sheepherders. Their flocks on the old Spanish land grants south of the Gila River numbered between 50,000 and more than 500,000 for a century and a half. The records of the state of Arizona in 1896 tell us that "every running stream and permanent spring were settled upon, ranch houses built and adjacent ranges stocked." Eventually, the ecology of this fragile, arid land collapsed under the weight of the cattle boom. The big cattle drives out of Texas and Sonora, Mexico coincided with a triple disaster in the 1880's: earthquakes and drought, followed by catastrophic floods that cut deep arroyos in the plains. Overgrazing had upset the balance among animal and grass and soil. The soil eroded away, leaving a "ruined land." The water-table fell. The rivers vanished.

If you travel the old coach road along the Mexican border, you won't see any cattle now. At one point there is a sign which reads: "60 miles — No Water," and the well on a deserted ranch is a welcome oasis. Nearby, the grave of a prospector is marked with an iron cross. The land has been reclaimed by the wilderness; by bighorn sheep that still come to water in the mountains; and by the Air Force, which uses one section as a bombing and gunnery range.

For the most part, the plants that grow back on an overgrazed desert range are the creosote bush, which is not palatable to many wild or domestic animals, and locoweed, which is poisonous to sheep. Recently about 1,200 sheep died from eating this weed in the Nevada corner of the Mojave.

33

The Cold Desert

Pungent silver sagebrush dominates the cold desert biome, centered in the upper Great Basin of northern California, Nevada, Oregon and Idaho. Much of this country, too, has been overgrazed in the past. And on the antelope refuges (Sheldon and Hart Mountains), the present cattlemen are allowed to graze their herds only under the strict regulation of the Government refuge manager. Outside of the refuges, thousands of acres are managed and leased for cattle only, under the U.S. Bureau of Land Management.

What plant dominates the cold desert?

In this semi-arid land, there has never been enough water to go around — even though the climate is cooler and slightly more predictable than in the Southwest (about five to ten inches of precipitation can be expected each year). Because the region is completely locked inside two great mountain ranges — the Rockies on the east and the Sierra of California on the west — drainage is poor. Rivers flowing out of these mountains end up in lakes or desert "sinks" where the salt and other minerals settle. The shallower lakes eventually dry up and turn into gleaming white salt flats.

What happens to desert lakes when they dry up?

One large, wild and beautiful lake, Pyramid Lake in northwestern Nevada, is an example of what happens when man comes to live in the desert and claims his share of the scarce water.

What was Pyramid Lake named for?

The lake, named for the great pyramid-shaped rock on its eastern shore, was discovered by Captain John Freemont in 1844. At that time the lake abounded in giant cut-throat trout, perch and many other kinds of fish. There were ducks and geese in great numbers. White pelicans nested on Anaho Island, also near the eastern shore, the largest colony of pelicans in all of North America. Paiute Indians made their living here, principally by fishing, even after the white men came into the area. It was, and still is, their lake — their reservation.

Between two and three months old, these young white pelicans cluster on the rocks of Anaho Island overlooking a dwindling channel — the protective moat between them and the mainland. Pyramid Lake, Nevada, has been receding since 1905.

What has happened to Pyramid Lake?

But in 1905, the Federal Government thought it would be a good idea to build a dam and divert the Truckee River, the source of the lake's water. The diversion canals took the water into a new town—Fallon, Nevada—where farmers had been encouraged to settle. Fallon became an oasis in the desert, an expanse of green garden. The farmers flourished, and the lake began to drop. So did the numbers of animals that depended on the water. Since the dam was built, the lake has dropped seventy feet. Trout that could once travel up the Truckee River to spawn, died out; the Indians' fishing business also died. (Today the trout in the lake are stocked, for sport only.) The primitive lakesucker called the cui-ui, found only in Pyramid Lake, still manages to spawn at the old river mouth but this fish too is endangered.

Ducks and geese, and the peregrine falcons that fed off them, are gone, and the number of white pelicans on Anaho has dropped from about 20,000 to 8,000 birds.

Where do the pelicans have to feed in summer?

Now the pelicans are faced with more threats to their very existence. Because the lake is so much lower, the adults can no longer feed at the river mouth past the late spring. It becomes a sand bar. They must fly some thirty miles to the Stillwater Wildlife Refuge in Fallon, to catch enough fish to feed themselves and their young.

The refuge contains hidden dangers. To protect their crops from destruction by insects, the farmers of Fallon spray their fields with chemical pesticides and the run-off enters the refuge through drainage ditches. DDT and the other pesticides used on the farms are ingested by the fish which are eaten by the pelicans. Depending on the concentrations in the bodies of the fish, and how many are eaten, the DDT, DDD, dieldrin and other formulations that were meant to kill only the insects can now kill the adult pelicans or their young.

Another threat to the pelicans is the rapid decline of the lake. If the water level drops another 15 feet — and unless it rains a great deal, this is very possible in the next dozen years — a land bridge will be exposed from the mainland to the southeastern tip of Anaho Island. If this happens, predators like the coyote, the bobcat and the fox will be able to walk onto the nesting grounds during the spring and kill all of the babies (which are then flightless and helpless) or eat the eggs.

What does sonic boom do to the pelican eggs and babies?

As if this threat to the eggs and young is not enough, another chapter in man's progress might just finish off the white pelicans of Anaho.

At Walker Lake Naval Air Base, just south of Pyramid Lake, there is a squadron of jet aircraft. The pilots of these planes fly over Anaho Island at speeds that cause sonic boom. When this is done around May or June, the adults fly off the nests, leaving their newly hatched babies and unattended eggs exposed to the hot sun — and worse, to the colony of western gulls that also nest on the island. The gulls have apparently learned to associate the sonic boom (which doesn't seem to scare *them*) with food. They take to the sky in hordes and come into the pelican rookeries to eat the babies and break the unhatched eggs. (The author witnessed the destruction of 40 nests after a sonic boom nearly knocked over the blind from which he was photographing the life cycle of the pelicans.)

Because man is in the desert to stay, there won't ever be enough water to go around for his crops, the fish, the pelicans and other animal life. It's very difficult to solve these problems when man's form of "progress" inevitably destroys, often without forethought or intention to kill. An irrigation project, a faster plane — these mark a kind of progress that the desert cannot withstand.

Grand, Middle, and South Tetons as seen reflected in a clear glacial pool from an unusual observation point on the western slope.

The Mountains

Due to the rugged nature of the mountain biome, man's imprint on the land has been less noticeable. Mountains are formidable—high, cold, steep, difficult to build in and hard to get through. And yet man's presence is being felt more and more in this remote, last frontier. Why? Here is the timber for our houses; the iron, coal, manganese and all the other materials to build the machinery of our civilized world.

What does man take out of the mountains?

To get all of these materials, man has built machines out of the very stuff of which the mountains are made. Two of the most destructive tools (or beneficial, depending on your point of view), are the bulldozer that hacks out roads and the helicopter.

37

When did the Western mountains start to rise?

In North America the highest mountain ranges are in the West. The Rockies run almost the entire length of the continent from Alaska to Mexico. Pushed up from a giant inland sea by gigantic upheavals within the earth some 135,000,000 years ago, these mountains have risen to heights of over 14,000 feet and some of the ranges are still rising today. To the west of the Rocky Mountains, the steep granite wall of the Sierra Nevada runs almost the length of the state of California.

The Southern Cascades of northern California, Oregon and Washington are mostly volcanic cones. Mt. Rainier (14,410 feet) stands like a sentinel over the broad plains of central Washington. Mount Rainier National Park, totally encompassing the mountain, occupies 378 square miles. Half a dozen or so major volcanoes have all been more or less active during the past century.

Mount Rainier in Washington is a huge volcanic cone, whose slopes are gouged by forty glaciers. Some, like Nisqually, shown here, are still active. The tip of the tongue of descending ice is hundreds of feet high.

When were the last volcanic eruptions in the West?

The last big eruptions occurred at Mt. Lassen, in California, in 1914 and again in 1915. The Northern Cascades of Washington form a distinct chain, with one great volcano, Mt. Baker, standing apart from the mountains near the Canadian border. Here, peaks only about 9,000 feet high are as jagged as the high Sierra or the majestic Teton Range of the Rockies. Few roads cut through this vastly glaciated, almost impenetrable wilderness.

Although these mountain chains are geographically different, they have many things in common. Much of the plant and animal life is the same. Differences may occur because a plant or animal has become isolated from the rest of its kind during the millions of years of mountain-building and the thousands of years of glaciation. Where huge valley glaciers have chiseled out the peaks, today there are only remnants — smaller glaciers and snow fields. One unique survivor is a flower, the James Boykinia (named for its discoverer), which grows only in the Olympic Mountains of Washington, and only on the sheerest of granite walls. Possibly the plant once grew in other places. Possibly its niche was broader than the cliffs, and over the years it retreated there to avoid being eaten by squirrels or mountain sheep or goats.

Because the Olympic Peninsula lies in a coastal fog belt, this is a unique area. At least 12 feet of snow fall each year on the peaks. (The highest, Mt. Olympus, is just under 8,000 feet.)

Mammoth glaciers push their way down into rain forest valleys facing the sea. Here, with 130 inches of rain a year, the Douglas fir and Sitka spruce grow bigger than any other trees on the continent, except the redwoods of California. Moist and eerie, the Olympic forest is completely draped with goat's-beard moss, not unlike the Spanish moss in the Florida swamps.

What is the tundra?

The treeless tops of mountains are called the tundra. Here there is not enough soil or moisture for anything to grow except shrubs and a mossy mat of miniature plants. You can find many of the same flowers that grow at lower elevations, such as forget-me-nots and Indian paint brush, but they're dwarfed and grow in bunches like desert plants, with thick and leathery leaves. The growing season is short because the snows of the tundra areas don't melt until mid-June and new snows can start as early as August.

Why are ptarmigan able to live here all year?

During this time, white-crowned sparrows, American pipits and horned larks are among the small birds nesting in the tundra gardens, but they leave as soon as the young are able to fly. The white-tailed ptarmigan is a year-round resident. In late spring, as the shrubs leaf out, the females molt into their brown plumage and become almost invisible while sitting on their eggs under the low plants. Males, still pure white, molt later in the summer. Then in the fall, both sexes change back into white feathers that blend perfectly with the snow.

All winter long the ptarmigan flocks wander in search of food. Long toe-feathers serve as snowshoes, and their sharp claws are useful for uncovering the vegetation beneath the drifts. Now they can find nothing to eat except the dormant buds of shrubs. With the opening of the buds in the spring, they quickly change their diet to green leaves, insects and spiders. Later there are berries and seeds, and so the cycle continues from year to year.

Ptarmigan babies are precocious — that is, they are born fully-feathered and begin to feed almost immediately by themselves. Within twelve hours after hatching, the hen will lead them away from the nest, abandoning any eggs that show no signs of life.

Since nature has protected the mother and young so well, it seems unfair that the father must keep his white feathers for so long after the snow has melted. The cock, now conspicuous against the green-turning land, is more vulnerable than his mate to attack by the golden eagles that hunt the high tundra.

King of the mountains — the golden eagle is the largest of the predatory birds on the tundra. The female, which is larger than the male, has a wingspan of some six and a half feet and may weigh about twelve pounds.

Because it is tiny and protectively colored, like the rocks of its habitat, a pika reveals its presence most often by its voice — a plaintive sound, much like a baby's cry.

Eagles also hunt two other permanent residents of the tundra and mountain meadows, the marmot and the pika. The marmot, a rodent which can weigh up to 20 pounds, inhabits the grassy Alpine meadow where it digs a deep hole for its den. The pika, a member of the rabbit family, weighs only four to six ounces, and lives in the talus slopes, the rock slide areas.

What else do eagles hunt on the tundra?

The reason both of these animals can live in what humans would consider a harsh environment is that they have evolved ways of coping with the long winter season.

The clear, loud whistle of the marmot echoes across mountain valleys. Along hiking trails, the great lumbering animals often station themselves on rock ledges and bask in the sun.

Around the beginning of August, the pika becomes very busy, cutting the stalks of the Alpine grasses and carrying them by the bundle to the entrance of its den in the rocks. Here the grasses are laid out to cure in the sun. When ripened, they are gathered and stored so that this little animal will have a supply of food during the winter.

How does the pika prepare for winter?

The marmot sleeps through the entire winter, so its method of preparation is different. It eats the grasses and stores them up in the form of animal fat, which is burned off slowly by its body during hibernation. Having gone to sleep a fat animal, it will wake up lean and hungry in the spring.

How does the marmot spend the winter?

Bigger mammals come to the Alpine meadows and tundras of the high mountains each year. In June, when it becomes hot in the lower valleys, the deer, elk, and mountain sheep and goats all migrate up to the cooler, higher places where the snows are melting, new grasses are growing, and the shrubs and trees are just coming into bloom. Here they feed until the heavy snows start to fall. (Snow "showers" are not unusual in July.) They will then migrate down to the lower valleys, where the snow is not so deep and food can be found.

How high trees can grow on a mountain depends on the latitude and sometimes special weather conditions. In New Mexico, treeline starts at about

What is treeline?

12,000 feet. Further north, in the Central Rockies, trees start to appear only at around 10,000 to 11,000 feet. In the Northern Rockies of Montana and British Columbia, treeline drops to below 8,000 feet (and to about 6,000 feet in our Pacific Northwest, due to the heavy snows and the big glaciers which cover the high slopes and invade the lower ones). Around Mt. McKinley in Alaska, no trees can survive at elevations above 3,000 feet.

Why are the evergreens at treeline small? The timber at treeline is, for the most part, a dwarfed forest of cold and drought-resisting evergreens. Lack of moisture and the short growing season may allow for only millimeters, not inches, of growth in a year. A tree with a diameter of six inches which is only five or six feet tall could be hundreds of years old.

How do aspen trees grow? Walking down a mountain, you go through different types of forest. In Colorado, below the wind timber, the same evergreens grow taller and straighter, forming a dark, closed woodland. At about 9,000 feet the spruce frequently opens up into sunny aspen forest. The quaking aspen is an interesting tree. Its flexible trunk bends, but seldom breaks, under the weight of the snow. The tree is deciduous, having delicate leaves that tremble in the wind but hold tenaciously to the branches until autumn. Then they turn pure gold and fly off, to settle on the forest floor or float down the streams. The aspen grows fast, and disasters that destroy the evergreens — fires or avalanches — give this tree more living space. It spreads quickly into the disaster area by means of auxiliary roots, or runners. There may be a dozen trees growing from one root system. Unlike the evergreen forest, the aspen woodland has grassy meadows in which deer browse, and are hunted by their main predator, the mountain lion. In about 20 or 30 years, the evergreens will grow back, closing the forest once more.

Below the aspen, between 6,000 to 9,000 feet, the Western yellow or ponderosa pine is the most prevalent tree. And below these pines, all along the front ranges of the Rockies, there are high grass plains.

But in the plateau country of the Southwest and the Great Basin deserts, juniper (sometimes called cedar) and piñon pine intervene between the mountain forests and the open sagebrush or grass plains. Lower still, in the Southwest, we would again find ourselves in the hot desert basins.

Though the plant life varies up or down the side of a mountain, its life zones are used by many of the same kinds of animals, moving up or down with the seasons, as food and living places become available.

What happens to a forest when it is lumbered? After the Eastern forests were cut over in the late 1800's, the lumbermen moved out to the Western mountains. Here spruce, fir, pine and redwood began to fall to the call of "Timber!" Beginning with the big Douglas fir and Sitka spruce of the mountains of

Washington and Oregon, the lumber companies gradually cut their way down through California, leaving desolation behind. For many years these lumber companies have stated in their ads, in magazines and on TV, that their practices have helped the forest by letting in the sunlight, and creating new niches for wildlife.

The trouble with the lumber industry's statement is that the same process, the opening of forest areas, happens naturally through fire and windfall and old age. But natural forest openings usually do not cover areas as extensive as those that men have cleared — thousands of square miles.

What happens to a forest when trees fall naturally?

Another difference between the natural opening-up of a forest and clear-cutting is that the minerals and chemicals in the trees do not return to the soil if they are cut down and hauled off to be sold commercially.

Most of the old timber that is still available for cutting in the West stands on public lands managed by the National Forest Service. Millions of acres are left in the remote Northern Cascade Mountains. In a recent study of land-use practices in the Cascades, investigators found that the Forest Service had allowed less clear-cutting during the past decade, recognizing the damage done in the past. The study team recommended continuation of block-cutting, which affects smaller areas, or selective cutting of certain trees.

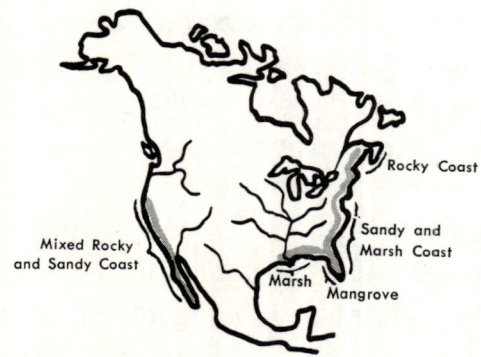

The Coastlines

The coastline of the North American continent is often considered to be the harshest—that is to say, the most inhospitable — of all the biomes. Although parts of a coastline vary, being sandy, marshy or rocky, the plant and animal life must be able to survive both in and out of water for hours at a time each day in a schedule governed by the tides.

How do coastlines vary?

The coastal organisms of the rocks have stationed themselves with all kinds of natural guy ropes and glues in three life zones, depending on their ability to exist out of water. Since the high tide zone is without water and exposed to sun and wind for more than half a day, this area is populated by the most drought-resisting species.

How many tidal life zones are there?

On the Maine coast, white barnacles mark the reach of high tide and seaweeds darken the low-tide area. Between these limits live shore organisms of the mid-tide zone.

What is a lichen? Dark lichens encrust the highest tide line. Not one plant, but two, the lichens are composed of fungi and algae in a symbiotic partnership. In this cooperative arrangement, the fungi hold onto rocks and absorb water and minerals with their filamentous roots while the algae carry on photosynthesis for the growth of the combined organism.

How do acorn barnacles feed? Just below are the thousands of white shells of the acorn barnacles. They are crustacean relatives of the lobster and have the ability to close their six-plated shells, retaining enough moisture to live while waiting for the next submergence. When a barnacle is underwater, two of the plates open and its feathery net gathers up the tiny plankton, the microscopic plants and animals of the sea, which it eats.

Where the tidal waters cover the rockweeds, mid-tide zone begins. The plant and animal community of this life zone can only be out of water for half a day or less. Here the colorful, flower-like anemone attaches itself to the sides of sea caves, or occupies open tidal pools.

A carnivorous creature, the anemone catches copepods (tiny crustaceans), baby fish, snails, anything that happens to touch its octopus-like tentacles, which close over the prey quickly. The food is sucked into the gut, where all but the indigestibles, such as shells, are consumed. The animal expels these through the same gut opening. Although anemones seem to be stationary, they can crawl around slowly on their stalks, just as the snails move from place to place.

What is symbiosis? In the dim interior of a cave, all the anemones are white; in the sunlight, they are colorful (the West Coast variety is a shimmering blue-green). The colors come from symbiotic algae within the animal. In this unique plant-animal relationship, the algae receive carbon dioxide, a waste product of the anemone's life processes, while the anemone uses oxygen, a by-product of the algae's photosynthesis, to "burn" food within its tissues. Both benefit from the association, which can only take place in sunlight. But the algae, completely contained and protected, have a slight advantage, as the anemone must still obtain some of its oxygen from the surging tides.

Second in size to the anemones of the Great Barrier Reef of Australia, our West Coast species, the green anemone, grows up to a foot in diameter. Its powerful tentacles, with a suction of 15.6 pounds per square inch, can capture a small fish.

Why are coastlines rich in life? In the lower zone, many kinds of seaweeds provide hiding places for the ocean's creatures. Under the lacy fronds and long, dripping wet blades of the weeds, the crabs and other animals are kept moist while the tide is low and the sun is hot. None is out of the water for very long.

From tide line to tide line, all living things sort themselves out according to their water needs. Even the young organisms, cast on the tides, return to their proper levels to mature — or they will die. Each has its place, ecologically.

Compared to the shore, the open sea is a kind of desert. Only along the edges of continents do rivers deposit their sediments and deep currents well up from the bottom of the ocean, supplying minerals for the growth of the plankton, which fishes eat. In the mud flat and marsh areas adjacent to the bays and deltas, ocean fish come in to spawn, and their young grow up in the protected nurseries. Here they can hide among the dense vegetation — comparatively safe from predators till they grow large enough to enter the more hostile ocean.

Why are we losing our fish supply? In recent years, two problems have upset the ecology of the shoreline that directly affect us. The first problem is land developers. In many of the coastal states around the country, these developers have come in to dredge up the marsh nurseries for housing developments. They dig up hundreds of miles of tidal marsh grasses. Massachusetts has lost about 20 per cent of its tidelands; Connecticut, nearly 50 per cent; New York, more than 30 per cent; and the other states aren't far behind. Eventually, many of us may have houses with a view of the sea but, in the process, we will lose part of our food supply — bluefish, sea trout, flounder, striped bass, redfish and many other fish which depend on these estuaries.

Why are pesticides not working?

The second problem facing us is the pollution of our coastal waters with chemical pesticides, such as DDT, which enter the seas through runoff from fields and rivers. When these chemicals were first used on our crops to kill the pest insects, they worked well. Now they do not, for a variety of reasons.

All members of the same species are not exactly alike, either in outward appearance or chemical content. Some people can be cured with penicillin, but others become very ill when they are given the same drug. Different reactions to the same drug are caused by chemical differences within the body. Similarly, not all individuals of a target species of insect can be killed by the same kind of spray.

Pest insects that attack our food crops are extremely prolific. They breed many times during a season, giving birth to literally billions of their kind. Since our crops are often planted in the thousands of acres, these pests breed astronomically in proportion to the large food supply.

Predatory or parasitic insects that feed on the pests are not as prolific. (If they were, they would eat up their entire food supply and starve to death.)

To protect his crops against these hordes of insects, the farmer sprays, and this may kill 99 per cent of the pests. One per cent might be different chemically. For them, it is not poison, and they produce generations of insects that we say are "resistant." To counter their resistance, the farmer sprays oftener, or uses stronger poisons. But the insects, with their great reproductive capacity, are still ahead of the technologists. Meanwhile, the war against them becomes increasingly expensive.

Problems and Alternatives

How does DDT spread through food chains?

The tragedy is that DDT and other chlorinated hydrocarbons that are 50 to 100 times stronger can kill other living things besides insects. Having been used for so many years in nearly every country in the world, the quantities of DDT in the environment are unbelievable — scientists estimate that a billion pounds of this chemical have now accumulated in the soil and water. It lasts for a long time — about 20 years. It does not kill directly, but passes through food chains from plant to animal to other animals, and is stored in the tissues.

The effects are now being seen in many places, particularly fresh and saltwater environments that receive agricultural runoff. In California, the entire coastline is in imminent danger of dying.

One source of contamination is the Oxnard Plain, where more than half of all the broccoli and celery and other truck crops in California are grown. DDT and other poisons sprayed here drain into the Santa Clara River, which flows into the Santa Barbara Channel. The DDT clings to bits of algae that are eaten by fish. The fish store the DDT in their tissues, especially the fatty tissues. These fish are eaten by larger predatory fish, and the DDT is transferred to them. Brown pelicans are among the sea birds that eat the larger fish, such as mackerel. All along the food chain the concentrations of the poison multiply. So the birds are the prime recipients.

As though on water skis, this adult brown pelican comes in for a landing. Because of their failure to raise young in recent years, these birds are becoming extinct in the United States.

What is happening to birds' eggshells?

This load of chlorinated hydrocarbons changes chemically in the pelicans' bodies into DDE, which hampers the manufacture of calcium. Eggshells are made of calcium, and during the breeding season, the females produce eggs with shells so thin that just sitting on the nests causes breakage. In 1969, the six hundred pairs of brown pelicans nesting on Anacapa Island were able to raise only five babies. And in 1970, only one egg hatched.

What is happening to pelicans in the U.S.?

What are the ecological implications of the loss of these birds? If there are no new young pelicans to replace the adults as they grow older and die off, the species will become extinct. (A previous decline along the Texas Gulf and Louisiana coasts for the same reason makes extinction on a continent-wide basis even more likely.)

It is now known that nearly all of the other species of sea birds that nest along the California Coast are affected in the same way. They lay eggs that may last for a day or so, but the normal movement of a parent in the nest smashes the thin-shelled eggs. Murres and some other sea birds normally have thicker shells, but even these are becoming thinner.

What effect is DDT having on seals?

The biologists' concern is underscored by their recent discovery that the California sea lions on the Channel Islands contain large amounts of DDT and DDE, which may account for the increasing numbers of seal young that are being born dead, prematurely.

Unusual parental behavior, possibly due to the effects of DDT on the nervous system, has also been observed in both the birds and the mammals. They may either desert their young, or fail to take care of them properly.

Though the U.S. Government watches the legal limits of the poisons in the fish that we eat, no one really knows what the side-effects in human beings of accumulating quantities might be.

Conservationists believe that we should not take a chance on destroying all of this life, and possibly ourselves as well. They are seeking a complete ban on the use of the hydrocarbon pesticides. Our agricultural scientists are divided between those who say we need the poisons to protect our food supply and those who argue that there are other alternatives. These alternatives hinge on using ecological knowledge to control the pest insects with a combination of less harmful chemicals (when necessary), special cultivation practices, and biological control. After all, they say, nature had been controlling itself for millions of years before man ever came on the scene. We could use the so-called beneficial insects — the predators and parasites — to control the insects that eat the crops.

What is biological control?

In California, citrus fruit is a major crop. Oranges, grapefruit and lemons are attacked by many insects. One in particular, the red scale, attaches itself to the skin of the fruit and sucks out the juices. Many hundreds of scale insects can infest a single orange, making it unsalable. If enough oranges are ruined, the farmer may even go out of business. To prevent this damage, he hires a chemical company to spray the groves.

Another farmer in the same area has discovered that spraying is no longer effective, and he has turned to biological control as a means of protecting his crop. When problems arise, he calls a commercial insectary. Their specialists might recommend the use of a tiny parasitic wasp called *Aphytis melinus,* which is no bigger than the head of a pin. What the female wasp does is to drill a hole through the waxy covering of the scale insect. She inserts her ovipositor and lays an egg on the scale's body. When the baby wasp hatches, it eats up the scale.

What does a parasite do?

The results of biological control have been excellent. In Fillmore, California, a farmers' cooperative even raises its own wasps. Together, its members own nine thousand acres of citrus on which little or no spray has been used during the past eleven years. They raise as much fruit on their land as the farmers who subscribe to chemical spraying programs, and at far less cost. Biological control costs about $25 per acre per year, while spray programs cost $100 per acre per year.

Does biological control work?

Speaking of cost, let us consider the total cost of a chemically sprayed orange, which costs us more to buy because someone must pay for the spray, namely, the consumer. But that's just a small part of the picture. One of the principles of ecology is: you can't change something without side-effects.

The point is that we do have alternatives, but only if we understand that we are part of the animal community, subject to the same laws that govern all life: diatom ... worm ... fish ... bird ... and man. It has been just a few years now since the words "ecology" and "pollution" have become part of our everyday language. Until recently, people just couldn't see the connection between the pollution of the environment, the loss of eagles and grizzly bears and other wild things, and their own survival. Now, hopefully, we are beginning to see that man, the animal, is *part* of the total complex life system on earth; that man, too, is one of the endangered species.

What can we do to stop pollution?

This is our concern now — that we clean our air and our water, that we protect ourselves from the chemical pesticides and find new ways to safeguard our crops. But we cannot succeed without knowing how these life systems work. This is ECOLOGY.

Will this little heron survive? Minutes out of the egg, its chances are already reduced by the fact that its parents have probably eaten contaminated fish, and the pesticide passes to the egg and the young.